I0475529

2Steps2Best

by Anthony Zolezzi

© 2015 Anthony Zolezzi
ISBN 978-1-329-77811-5

First printing: December, 2015

A Note From Anthony

I like people. I like talking with them — the exchange of ideas, the interaction. I get a lot out of simply getting to know someone and finding out about their hopes and aspirations. I guess that's natural, coming from a big, Italian family like I do. And it's in these exchanges, sometimes with complete strangers, that I've realized... we all have the potential to do amazing things in our own life.

I've been very fortunate to live a fantastic life. I've been able to live, for most of my life at least, in a way that reflects my true passions. Now, understand, it wasn't always an easy ride! And I didn't always have my head together, but once I came to understand what my passion and purpose in this life are, well, let's just say things began to fall into place for me. And I want to do anything I can do to help you live with purpose and abundance, too.

Over the years, I've been fortunate enough to work with some amazing people. Many of those with whom I've worked have kept in touch with me and we've actually ended up working together again and again. This has happened so often in fact, that I like to call the group "the team."

The team is made up of some of the best partners I've ever worked with. We've come together to create and nurture many companies, from the Bubba Gump Shrimp Co. to GreenOpolis Recycling, Pet Promise pet food, Wild Oats Foods, and even our latest endeavor, a 21st century reboot of S&H Green Stamps.

For some years now, whenever I talk with people about their hopes for their lives, I've answered questions about this business or that project that I've been involved in. I've always wanted to be able to give them a concise answer when they ask me how I've accomplished the things I have been able to accomplish.

One day I realized, there are really only two steps that have led me to this purpose and passion. I realized there were two steps that helped me create the path Those two steps came from an ancient Zen proverb which states — Before Enlightenment, Chop Wood And Carry Water. After Enlightenment, Chop Wood And Carry Water.

In my mind, I immediately called it 2Steps2Best. I started to live by this simple dictum, and I was amazed by the abundance I found.

This ebook is my way of explaining what those two steps— "chop wood and carry water" — are in more detail, because I want you to be able to experience this abundance in your life.

If you are reading this, it's highly likely that we've met and I directed you to 2Steps2Best. I hope there is a morsel in here that helps you. And, if you stumbled on this book by accident or even if a friend told you about it, remember one thing as you read this ebook …that you are awesome and extraordinary and if you chop wood and carry water every day you will feel it every day. And your life will begin to show it, every day.

Rock On—

Anthony

Introduction

2Steps2Best contains a blueprint to help you achieve the abundance and meaning we are all looking for in life. Through 2Steps2Best, you will be able to find the balance that will allow you to uncover your true path. And 2Steps2Best will give you the tools to follow that path.

2Steps2Best is based on an ancient Zen proverb that is still relevant - and effective - today.

> *Before Enlightenment…*
> *Chop Wood And Carry Water.*

> *After Enlightenment…*
> *Chop Wood And Carry Water.*

But 2Steps2Best is not a book about Zen. It is a book about abundance. It is a book about how to apply this Zen proverb to your life and to your relationships and to your understanding of your work, to help you find a passion and a balance that will help you achieve the success you desire.

The essence of work and living comes down to two simple steps. Chop wood and carry water. Based on this idea - and through many years of practice and trials - I have developed the formula that I call 2Steps2Best. These are steps I do each day, every day. The two simple instructions contained in this 1000 year-old Zen proverb have had a profound effect on my life. Doing these two simple steps can change the direction of your life, too.

All you need to do is follow the guidelines I have set out in this e-book, and you will find the abundance you are looking for.

Focus On The Right Steps

If you focus on the right steps, you can create change and draw abundance to you.

What is abundance? For me, abundance is success. And abundance is gained through passion and purpose. Through chopping wood and carrying water, I learned what my passion and my purpose are in this world. And though developing my passion and pursuing my purpose, I have gained abundance and joy.

Thousands of years after *Before Enlightenment Chop Wood And Carry Water, After Enlightenment, Chop Wood And Carry Water* was first uttered, this concept for abundance - and ultimately survival - is the same. Every day we need to chop wood and carry water - even though we have heating systems in our home and most have running water. The key here is that we have to be mindful of the work we have to do to be successful. For each of us to be successful at whatever we do, we must perform these two acts every day.

This realization hit me— even though I didn't know it at the time— that as CEO of Pacific Basin Foods and Fresh Connection and even as a turnaround specialist, I had been chopping wood and carrying water.

Just by chopping wood and carrying water every day, my personal passion and sense of purpose had bubbled up and made the meaning of all my activities much clearer. And if you begin to chop wood and carry water, you will have a similar epiphany. Mine ultimately became about working on the side of the angels in whatever wood I chopped or water I carried, and that has morphed into a kind of lifelong mission.

If you mindfully chop wood and carry water, if you understand these actions— feel them— you will discover your own true passion and purpose. Following these principals will give you rewards that are truly remarkable. You will find abundance and joy as you pursue your own passion and purpose.

The Day I Discovered Chop Wood And Carry Water

There was a time in my career when I was doing a turnaround of a large company, having
just sold my second start-up at 36. I had no formal turnaround experience but I was cocky and young, so I arranged meetings with turnaround experts Sandy Sigoloff, Richard Giegeline and Charles Lynch.

After learning their language, I decided that was what I wanted to do, so I put that on my office door – Anthony Zolezzi, TurnAround Artist, and, amazingly, within a few months had accomplished my first turnaround engagement, making more money than I could ever imagine.

I jumped in and worked at it every day, 7 days a week, really pushing myself, but what I didn't like were all of the firings and dismantling it involved.

So did it succeed? Let's just say I broke it down and sold the parts -- in the company's mind, I stemmed the loss of millions of dollars every month, but in my mind, at a real personal and human cost.

Despite that, I jumped right into another turnaround because I felt like I was on a roll and making a lot of money and, honestly, it was somewhat intoxicating -- but it wasn't fun this time at all, and I knew it wasn't what I wanted to do.

So when a particular job on behalf of Bank of America was complete, I went to Mexico and really evaluated my options.

Two things came out of this trip. One thing was that I decided I did not want to do this type of work at the expense of the people — it wasn't me, and making money this way wasn't me, either.

But what really "turned me around" was reading the stack of books I took along – or, maybe I should say, my wife, who was into life's more spiritual aspects, took along for us to read.

That day I read the ancient proverb…

Before Enlightenment
Chop Wood And Carry Water

After Enlightenment
Chop Wood AndCarry Water

That just stood me right up from my chair, and walking down the beach, I kept repeating chop wood and carry water, chop wood and carry water.

Then I thought, of course, in a primitive society, you have to chop wood every day for warmth and the ability to cook food for the family, and you have to carry water for the family to drink and bathe, and this needs to be done every day. So chopping wood was the action that you need to take every day to ultimately build a wood pile, and carrying water is what you do for everyone else close to you, and that if you do these on a daily basis, you will be rewarded with joy, abundance and success.

And when you continue to do it even after you've become enlightened, you will be putting yourself in a position to realize more of these than you ever thought possible.

Understanding The Principal

The basic premise is that both chopping wood and carrying water are critical to survival. In ancient times, chopping wood and carrying water were necessary because everyone needed wood to heat their home and cook, and water to drink and bathe. Chopping wood once meant literally swinging an axe to create a pile of wood that would be sufficient to provide for the needs of your family. Basically, chopping wood is the idea that you must do some type of productive work each day.

But to put it into context as an idea for gaining abundance — or success— chopping wood means taking action - not being afraid to swing the axe - to do the work you need to do each day to further your goals and move toward abundance. Just keep chopping each day, so one day you will get a wood pile.

Carrying water encompasses the idea that each day, we must help others in some way, so carrying water simply means doing something for someone else. For thousands of years it was carrying water for someone else. In fact, if you look around it even signifies doing something unpleasant on the behalf of someone else.

Now, again, to put this into context to help you move forward in your success, just do something for someone else every day. Yes, every day. And do it deliberately. You don't have to be Mother Teresa. It could be anything. Think about simplicity. Carrying water could be picking up the phone and calling someone and just saying hello and seeing if there is anything that you can do for them.

Carrying water could be giving the individual with the cardboard sign a dollar today. It's helping someone in some way each day. Absolutely anything for anyone else.

Now that you know what it means, you can begin to incorporate these principals into your life. You can begin to chop wood and carry water today, right now.

The Foundation: Chop Wood Every Day

As I've said, chopping wood is all about productivity. It is the idea that each day should be about accomplishing something that moves your idea of abundance forward in a real way.

Any goal, from losing weight to getting in shape, is an every day occurrence - not just once in a while. It is work. Conscious work. Work is accomplishing something, working towards building that wood pile. Every day .

Especially when it comes to your life's purpose, you might be thinking that chopping wood means sitting at your desk on your computer, working in a traditional way. But, anyone that thinks being in an office is the only way to work is wrong.

Now, if you're doing that in an office setting and you like it, great. But today, realize that anywhere you can think of that you'd like to work, you can work. For instance: at home, on the beach, even in your car. These days, work is more non-traditional. It's not about simply punching a clock and getting a pay check. It's more about reaching your potential. Doing something you're passionate about. Chopping wood doesn't have to be a conventional exercise. You never know when - or where - an important spark will come from. It's how you chop wood that is the key. Inspiration and insight can come from anywhere.

Some people would disagree, but I believe that meditating and thinking about a problem or how to accomplish something can be the most effective way to chop wood. Thinking about and deciding how to accomplish something or solve some problem is just as important as actually doing the work.

For instance, recently I had several key projects to write up and needed to focus my attention - versus sitting at my desk, stimulated by the 85 degree weather in March in San Diego! So I decided to hit the road and pick three locations. I decided to take a one-hour break at each stop and get my work done.

My first coffee shop stop was the Pannikin with an objective to outline an approach to the week for two key projects. Then the next stop was a Pete's Coffee and my goal was to write the key project outline then take a short walk through a farmers' market to clear my head. The last stop was a coffee shop called Positano. I think by now you are getting the point - that for chopping wood sometimes it is great to get into the forest in different places with different smells and different looks and feels. So next time you need to chop a lot of wood - compartmentalize and move - get a different look and feel and see if the point of view changes. If it does, rejoice - you might have chopped down a different tree.What You Do For Others:Carry Water Every Day

The second principle in 2Steps2Best is carry water. The entire secret of 2Steps2Best is chop wood and carry water every day. Now that you know what it means to chop wood, let's talk about what it means to carry water.

First, let me say that it is a fantastic feeling to carry water for whoever needs it. By carrying water, a sense of purpose becomes a really powerful, unstoppable way to attract abundance in all dimensions. When you finish carrying water, you should feel good about it. Carrying water, essentially, is doing something for someone else. It is the emotional side of the hard work of chopping wood. There are essentially no goals or objectives here - just a daily reminder to do one thing each day for someone else.

But, carrying water should also be consistent with your personal reason for being on this planet. It should fit into your overall plan for your life. Ask yourself if this act of carrying water or helping someone else is adding to your personal mission and your personal sense of purpose. This may sound selfish, but really it isn't.

When carrying water outside of your immediate family and friends, it's okay to choose activities for carrying water that reflect your larger goal.

For instance, If you're chopping wood to build a business in the sustainability field, you might consider giving of your time to help further clean water efforts. Or possibly get involved in recycling efforts in your community. This type of activity would go hand in hand with your personal objectives.

This type carrying water for others is productive on a larger scale, too. You are giving back, and it is mindful and purposeful. You are giving with intent. You will be coming full circle in your own life, bringing together your mission and purpose (chopping wood) while attending to the needs of others (carrying water).

Every day you should ask yourself what did you do for someone else. It is especially great when it is something that you did that that person would consider unpleasant. And just like chopping wood you have to be relentless in your approach to getting it done and checking that box every day.

Make sure that you also think about those close to you - your friends and family. It's easy to get caught up in the idea of helping others and spend all of your energy on those outside your immediate circle. But you will gain a sense of completeness when you give to those you love. Don't forget them. Make them a priority in your life.

The easiest way to carry water for those you love is simply ask them how they are doing, and really listen to what they say. You might be surprised by what you hear. And if you find out that they are going through something difficult, remember that you don't have to take some big, extravagant action, Being there for them, saying a kind word and listening is the best thing you can do for those you love.

Tell them you love them. Remind them how strong you think they are. Let them know that while you may not be able to fix whatever is wrong, you are with them, and will be with them as they go through this difficult time.
And don't forget to let them know that you are grateful to them for trusting you enough to share whatever is going on in their lives with you.

Unselfish giving to those you love is a reward in itself - outside of your personal mission. This is the type of carrying water that will bring a fullness to your life that you simply will not find in other areas. This act of kindness in carrying the water is enhanced by the power of family support.

In fact your family and friends' support of your success is critically important. I personally have made the mistake of not providing my family and friends the care and water carrying that I was giving to others. It became problematic and cost me my marriage, which I regret to this day.

You might think this part of the equation seems hard. I understand how you feel. Personally, I find it harder to carry water every day than to chop wood. Maybe because the competitive side of me is more comfortable with the chopping wood. Possibly because chopping wood is unemotional and the carrying water is emotional.

And, there's another important thing I want you to think about. Sincerity. Whatever you do, whether it is for your family or your community, you must do it with a sincere heart.

An act cannot be considered carrying water if it is not done from the heart. But, this skill can be learned. Think of carrying water as you would any muscle in your body. With use and exercise, you can learn to carry water successfully and sincerely. Don't invite the negative Karma that can develop if you are not sincere.

The Heart Of Abundance

Your unique purpose in the world can't be figured out with your overactive, thinking mind. Your mind isn't designed to know your soul's purpose. Your mind is designed to help you take action on achieving your dreams once you know where you're going.

So first, you must get to the heart of it.

Your purpose lives in your heart. It emerges from your heart. And when it emerges from your heart, you get chills. And that's the sign from the universe that you're on the right track. Then the worries about how it will make money subside. They don't go away, but they lessen. Because you just know what you HAVE to do, no matter what.

For anyone reading this, my recommendation is just pick the purpose that comes first to your mind. The idea that you feel comfortable with. Don't over think it and as you go through the process of chopping wood and carrying water adjust accordingly.

When you have a mission, a passion, a purpose - to share with the world - and you live in alignment with that mission, the universe conspires to support you on all levels. You will attract abundance just because you're living in the high vibrational feeling tone of your best self.

So, stop thinking and trying to figure it out. Relax. Take a yoga class. Travel to a beautiful location. Start drumming or singing. Live in the feeling tone of your perfect life right now! If you begin to do this, your true purpose will come to you. The idea, your passion and purpose, will come like a huge beautiful ocean wave and you won't be able to miss it. I want you to uncover your true potential and set a path toward that goal.

Live Abundantly

When people ask me what I am doing every day I say chopping wood and carrying water. Every day, Chopping wood. Every day. Carrying water. So, if you want abundance, you need to live in a way that will allow you to reach your goal. You need to live abundantly.

With regard to the first part of the equation— chopping wood— If you know what you want to accomplish, great! You're ahead of the game. But you may not know what your passion and purpose are just yet. That's okay, too. The important thing is to begin to live the idea of chopping wood and carrying water. By beginning to live in this way, you will find your passion and purpose.

But remember it is not a straight line. In fact, it is going to be a very rocky and curvy road with twists and turns you never thought of. You have to continue to push - think about chopping wood every day. You chop the wood and that night you burn it to keep you warm. The next morning you wake up and you have to start chopping again.

I want you right now, if you know what you want to accomplish, write it down. Its kind of old school, but I like it written down on paper. I just like the feel of the process of writing it down. It helps with the old genetic system we have of hand-eye coordination. And writing things down somehow makes them seem more concrete in my mind. If I write something down, I feel as if it's no longer simply an idea floating around, but a plan with substance and weight.

And every day, write down what you did on that day to push that agenda forward. If you don't know what you want to accomplish, begin by simply writing down what you've thought about. Think about what ideas have interested you, what you've taken the time to look into or researched.

I keep a to- do sheet like this with each project written on card stock and underneath, a list of the actions I took today or am going to take tomorrow. I don't let one day go by in which I don't accomplish one or more of the actions I've assigned myself.

My other recommendation for living abundantly has to do with carrying water. It's that famous admonition…

Always let your conscience be your guide
—Jiminy Cricket

That means, for example that you don't want to go cutting down the Brazilian rain forest for the purpose of chopping wood. It also means doing it mainly to benefit others, whether it's your loved ones or society as a whole. This was what first motivated me, many years ago, to learn the World Book Encyclopedia backwards and forwards – the pang of conscience I felt, even as a child, about wasting the money my father had labored so hard to bring in.

Always keep the happiness of those you value most uppermost in your mind – the same reason I recommend you call someone in the family and tell them you love them out of the clear blue. They might be surprised, but it will feel good, believe me.

And don't worry if the sense of purpose doesn't bubble up quickly -- just keep chopping wood and carrying water in the knowledge that the results will soon become.

You can begin today to move toward your goal, to move toward the abundance you want. But only you can do the work that is necessary to achieve you goals. The important thing is to move forward with your desire or idea every day. Begin to live abundantly every day.

Make A Commitment To Yourself

This journey started when I was 6 years old. My father was a fisherman who was out to sea during most of my formative early years making a living and working extremely hard. When I think about how hard he worked fishing with three of us children at home with my mom, it gives me chills. I clearly remember my mom was always aspiring to make sure we were taught something every day and that we were always inspired to learn and explore. So one day when she so proudly came home with the World Book Encyclopedia it was consistent with what she wanted for us and she was excited for us to dig in.

Well, the books kind of sat there unopened for a few months until my dad came home from fishing. I remember him getting rather upset about the expense of the World Book. He wasn't really mad so much as questioning the need for that big an expenditure when fishing was tough. Upon hearing that, I decided that for the family and my mom I better read the World Book Encyclopedia from A to Z. So that evening I started and in my mind I was going to stay up all night to get through the entire alphabet of topics. Well I started to read A and barely got through a few pages, and said, whew, I had no idea there was that much reading involved. So, the most important lesson I took from the World Book experience was that to accomplish this goal, I needed to read a little bit each day not overwhelm myself but just stay with it -- and that I did.

Within 9 months I had read the entire World Book Encyclopedia from A-Z (which was only fitting, considering my name) and I couldn't wait to tell my mom and dad, especially have my dad ask me a question about the Blue Whale or any other type of whale, for that matter, so I could give him the answer from the World Book Encyclopedia. And that's what I did. Then just for good measure I read it again, backwards, meaning from Z-A, which was much faster but involved the same exact method reading a little every day and rejoicing when there was large pictures.

Now, 20 years later, just like my approach to tackling that World Book, any start-up or new business or even a mountain climb or marathon takes the commitment to get going, whether it involves training or learning.

If you do something every day, even if it's just a Google search for something you need to know or a call to an expert or a physical workout – but keep at it, there's no telling what you might end up achieving. Dr Dre didn't build Beats to a $2 billion dollar check from Apple without this kind of resolve.

As Travis Kalanick, Uber CEO, told me earlier in a San Francisco meeting, I'm just ultra focused on the business. His company didn't get an $18 billion dollar valuation without daily wood chopping and carrying water in a way that has made the Uber experience a magical and delightful one for customers.

Chopping Wood And Carrying Water Every Day Takes Stamina

Now, just to add some texture to the ideas in this book, I want to remind you that it takes a lot of energy to chop wood and carry water. So make sure you start being mindful about your diet, the amount of exercise you get and the amount of sleep you get.

Chopping wood isn't necessarily a conventional exercise, but it takes stamina and energy as well as determination. Carrying water isn't necessarily a physical endeavor, but it requires mental focus and concentration.

Chopping wood can be physically exhausting and many times this first part of gaining abundance is exactly that you have to commit to working hard every day to achieve your goal.

Here's an example: I was in dire straits, absolutely failing as I worked on a turn around project for a $350 million dollar Seafood Company. The company's margins were declining rapidly and sales were on the downslide. It was 1994 - I just realized that was 20 years ago and man, was I a young punk then! But anyway, the company was in a bad way. I was failing miserably. So what did I do? I went to the movies! And it turned out to be one of the best moves I ever made.

After watching this particular movie - at an afternoon matinee - I went straight to Paramount Pictures the next morning and planted myself at the guard gate. I told myself I would stay right where I was until someone would see me about licensing The Bubba Gump Shrimp company name. And yes, after sitting outside the guard shack in the parking lot for almost 10 hours, at 6:30 pm Debbie P. asked me in.

An hour later life became art and the Bubba Gump Shrimp company was born - over 3500 retailers signed on to the program decorating their seafood sections as Bubba Gump Shrimp.

The Seafood Company's margins soared. Eventually, Con Agra bought it. The Company came out of bankruptcy - a company of which I had been a shareholder.

In the same way, carrying water requires your undivided attention. You must be present, you must be connected to your loved ones and the world around you to be able to sincerely give of yourself to others. To carry water effectively, you must be your best self, your healthiest self, your most authentic self.

So, what do you need to be able to chop wood and carry water at the top of your ability? As I said above, stamina and energy. Without these it will be nearly impossible to chop the wood you need each day, Let alone carry the water!

So what impacts your stamina and energy levels?

Three things: what we eat, how much we exercise and how well we sleep.

A human is different than an engine that just needs gasoline or electricity. We are more complex and therefore need mindfulness in the way we fuel our bodies to be at our most productive.

These three things, how you eat, how you sleep and the amount of exercise you get each day directly impact your ability to chop wood and carry water.

Here are a few key components to consider when choosing foods you'll eat.

If you become mindful of your diet, you will begin to eat whole healthy foods. What does that mean? Well, let me ask you a question...

How do you feel after you eat a bag of Cheetos or Fritos versus an apple, a bag of carrots or a green salad? Can you tell a difference?

If you can, then you already have a good idea of where I'm going with the idea of mindfulness. If you can't tell a difference, then the first place to start is to think about how you feel when you give your body healthy fuel as opposed to processed junk fuel. Becoming mindful is simply thinking about the choices you make when you fuel your body. Just the same as not putting sugar in the gas tank of your car if you want it to run properly, don't put junk into your body and expect it to run properly!

Think of it this way, research shows that processed foods are full of actual toxins - substances that are toxic to your body. These toxins act much like a hang-over, they take so much energy to process that they will make you feel slow and sluggish.

Here's another rule of thumb to guide you into mindful eating. Any word on the label that you don't recognize as food, like trans fat, modified corn starch, hydrolyzed, mono, tri, - are not real foods. These substances will make you sluggish.

The energy it takes to chop wood every day requires a clean diet. One of whole nutritious foods heavy in vegetables and protein. Clean protein like grass fed beef, and grass fed milk or goat milk products. Vegetables should be abundant in every meal - try and utilize different colored veggies to mix the nutrient content. On the fruit side, yes it's great for you, but make sure to eat the fruit that is in season with where you are.

Obviously whenever possible always eat organic because the pesticides in the food will slow you down. Your body has to take extra energy to fight off the toxins in the pesticides.

You can find a lot more about eating right on www.food-fit.org and www.foodguy.org as well as thedailyapple.com and DrGundry.com.

So, begin to be mindful about how you fuel your body. When you sit down to eat a meal, think, Out with processed and in with whole and natural.

Remember That Daily Exercise Is Crucial

Needless to say, you are going to have to be in good shape to chop wood every day so proper stretching and exercise is a must. These exercises can be random - in fact it's actually better if they are! Try not to get in the trap that I personally get in, which is doing the same routine every day. Try and mix it up - some yoga, some stretching, some strength. You also need some core exercises.

Simply walking every day for 40 minutes to an hour can have incredible energy stimulating characteristics. Having an exercise regime - any exercise at all - is really important in being able to chop wood. In fact, when I lived in Pennsylvania, I really did chop wood...for the exercise.

But most important, use your own body weight and mix it up. Recently I have been doing FitStar and have enjoyed the soreness of mixing it up. Also there are many free apps that will give you a varying degree of exercise. But, you must exercise. Keeping your body fine-tuned is important. Heavy weight and lack of exercise will - no pun intended - weigh on your ability to chop wood.

Get Enough Rest

The other most under-recognized key to giving you the energy to chop wood is how you rest, sleep and restore. Sleep is so important. Sleep is the time when all the cells of the body are healing and recharging. So if you aren't sleeping at least 8 hours per night, you won't have the necessary energy to chop wood each day. In other words, if you are burning the candle at both ends, you're not letting the cells repair and it will be much harder to chop wood and create that wood pile.

It is an absolute must that you rest and restore your cells every day through adequate sleep. When chopping wood and carrying water you have to always make sure you are in top shape. Besides eating good food, you have to get plenty of sleep. I personally try to get 10 hours whenever I can. But I tell people I work with that it is a minimum of 8. Now don't confuse this with induced sleep through sleeping pills. What I'm talking about is restorative sleep.

Simplify Your Life And Attract Abundance

We all want abundance. But the process of attracting that abundance to your life can feel overwhelming. Well, breathe. Settle your thoughts. Take a walk, meditate, or even see a movie. Inspiration can come from almost anywhere. And inspiration will lead you to your true passion and purpose, which will attract the abundance you are looking for.

I was recently reminded, while watching the video of Carlos Viejas Perez, the famous Uruguayan artist, that he inspired me to do more, to do it better, and to do it unconventionally. For me, if I can do projects that are good for the people and planet and inspire others to come along, then I am working within my personal sense of purpose.

Now, admittedly, I have gotten much better at chopping wood and carrying water over the past 20 years – you might even say I've become so much more enlightened during that time. But that enlightenment has only served to amplify the rewards I've realized in joy and abundance.

I find that when I talk with very successful people, there is always that same unrelenting passion to 'keep up the chopping and carrying'. Once you have 2Steps2Best in your possession, ask anyone that is successful if this was the formula, and they will all say yes, guaranteed!

The principals of chop wood, carry water have worked for me, and they will work for you, too. All you need to do is follow the guidelines I have set out in this e-book, and you will find the abundance you are looking for. It will work for whatever you want to accomplish - whether it's business-related or personal - these two simple steps will work for you.

I want nothing more than for you to find your abundance, your success. And that abundance is available to you — and everyone who wishes to pursue it — through the principals of 2Steps2Best.

Inspiration

Great quotes inspire us to change, to grow, and to become our best selves. I researched thousands of quotes from successful leaders for my last book, to capture one for each chapter, covering 11 simple concepts to become a better leader. My recent LinkedIn post explaining the 11 concepts became the 2nd most read article in LinkedIn history (at 1.3 million views!) So, I'm sharing my favorite quotes here- those which inspired me enough that I published them in the book, along with the runners up. Here are my 25 favorite likable leadership quotes. I hope they inspire you as much as they have inspired me:

Listening

*When people talk, listen completely. Most people never listen -
Ernest Hemingway*

The most basic of all human needs is the need to understand and be understood. The best way to understand people is to listen to them. - Ralph Nichols

Storytelling

Storytelling is the most powerful way to put ideas into the world today. -Robert McKee

If you tell me, it's an essay. If you show me, it's a story. —Barbara Greene

Authenticity

I had no idea that being your authentic self could make me as rich as I've become. If I had, I'd have done it a lot earlier. -Oprah Winfrey

Authenticity is the alignment of head, mouth, heart, and feet - thinking, saying, feeling, and doing the same thing - consistently. This builds trust, and followers love leaders they can trust. -Lance Secretion

Transparency

As a small businessperson, you have no greater leverage than the truth. -John Whittier

There is no persuasiveness more effectual than the transparency of a single heart, of a sincere life. -Joseph Berber Lightfoot

Team Playing

Individuals play the game, but teams beat the odds. -SEAL Team Saying

Alone we can do so little; together we can do so much. - Helen Keller

Responsiveness

Life is 10% what happens to you and 90% how you react to it. - Charles Swindoll

Your most unhappy customers are your greatest source of learning. - Bill Gates

Adaptability

When you're finished changing, you're finished. -Ben Franklin

It is not the strongest of the species that survive, nor the most intelligent, but the one most responsive to change. —Charles Darwin

Passion

The only way to do great work is to love the work you do. -Steve Jobs

I have no special talents. I am only passionately curious. -Albert Einstein

Surprise and Delight

A true leader always keeps an element of surprise up his sleeve, which others cannot grasp but which keeps his public excited and breathless. -Charles de Gaulle

Surprise is the greatest gift which life can grant us. - Boris Pasternak

Simplicity

Less isn't more; just enough is more. -Milton Glaser

Simplicity is the ultimate sophistication. -Leonardo daVinci

Gratefulness

I would maintain that thanks are the highest form of thought, and that gratitude is happiness doubled by wonder. -Gilbert K Chesterton

The essence of all beautiful art, all great art, is gratitude. -Friedrich Nietzsche

Leadership

Management is doing things right; leadership is doing the right things. — Peter F. Drucker

If your actions inspire others to dream more, learn more, do more and become more, you are a leader. —John Quincy Adams

Leadership and learning are indispensable to each other. —John F. Kennedy

Those are my favorite quotes. Now it's your turn. Which of these quotes speak most to you? What are your favorite quotes about abundance, leadership and success? And which qualities make you a likable leader? Let me know and here's to all of us finding abundance and joy!

www.ingramcontent.com/pod-product-compliance
Lightning Source LLC
Chambersburg PA
CBHW021855170526
45157CB00006B/2451